Coït

FIRST ENGLISH EDITION
original text copyright © 2012, Éditions La Peuplade et Chantal Neveu
English translation © 2012, Angela Carr
Originally published in French by La Peuplade, 2010
Note on The Text © 2012, Chantal Neveu, English translation © 2012 Angela Carr
Graphic Design: Jason Milan Ghikadis
Cover: Jay MillAr

All rights reserved. No part of this publication may be reproduced or transmitted
in any form or by any means, electronic or mechanical, including photocopying,
recording, or any information storage or retrieval system, without permission
in writing from the publisher.

The production of this book was made possible through the
generous assistance of The Canada Council for The Arts
and The Ontario Arts Council.

We acknowledge the financial support of the Government of Canada through the
National Translation Program for Book Publishing for our translation activities.

 Canada Council   Conseil des Arts   ONTARIO ARTS COUNCIL
for the Arts   du Canada   CONSEIL DES ARTS DE L'ONTARIO

LIBRARY AND ARCHIVES CANADA CATALOGUING IN PUBLICATION

Neveu, Chantal, 1964-
[Coït. English] Coït / Chantal Neveu ; Angela Carr, translator.

Translation of: Coït. A Poem.
ISBN 978-1-927040-39-3

I. Carr, Angela II. Title. III. Coït. English.

PS8577.E7597C6413 2012   C841'.54   C2012-905409-7

PRINTED IN CANADA

Chantal Neveu

Coït

Translated by Angela Carr

BookThug Toronto 2012

Dancing bodies go together.

Going together: *cum* (with) + *ire* (to go) – *coït* (coitus).

Through visible and invisible tubes: of bodies, in bodies, between bodies. With.

1	2	3	4	5	6	7	8	9

```
         1    2    3    4    5    6    7    8    9


I come in


           between

                                              tubes




                         in my tubes




                                   I can't see




from where I leave
I come in
```

you point to where you want me to enter

yes

I can show you

the key

entrances

elastic

scale variations

there

	1	2	3	4	5	6	7	8	9
I come in									
								I see	
		you do what							
		what							
		I want							
						gestures			
					openings				
								sensitive limits	
					hypersensitive				
		what							
								bodily	
						fictions			
		I don't know							

```
        1    2    3    4    5    6    7    8    9


            what I don't know

            what I want



when I come out you know where I was
                                                corridors
where I am no longer



            where this still tingles
                                                needles


in a way




                        shining

                            radiance
```

	1	2	3	4	5	6	7	8	9
you see									
after the gestures									
		your actions remain							
					localized				
							pulsing		
									deep in walking
					this heat persists				
								trembling	
							internally		

1　2　3　4　5　6　7　8　9

spaces tremble

columns of air

if we can do it

if we like

go together

                                    the skin also trembles

                                    intermittently

                                    the entire skeleton

                                    the flesh

                                                            red

            marks

                                                        deeds

                                    under the nails

                                    under the eyelids

                                    other tubes

                                                        unknown to me

	1	2	3	4	5	6	7	8	9

your nerves

one by one

                                                telescoping

                                                      reflexes

your genes

                                                                          every limb

                    mirror

neurons

                                                                     implicit nudity

        you see me

          across

                                   electric surfaces

	1	2	3	4	5	6	7	8	9

        how

                immersed

        you know

I feel you

                as deeply

                              relentlessly

                as withdrawn

                              I can see

        my fragile constitution

                              persistence

                                  particles
                                  of the whole

            limbs

                              I want to see everything

                    under the membranes

                              sonorous volumes

1	2	3	4	5	6	7	8	9
		what						
			this involves					
			a charge					
				contractions				
					bright	zones		
				turbulence				
						aberrations		
			biomechanical					
	piano							
							all	
							these fluid lines	
go ahead								
	non piano							
						bereft	of the	instrument

1	2	3	4	5	6	7	8	9
					X			
	what							
	I like							
	you know							
							what this involves	
			non-isometrical					
							the sounds	

intimate

to this extent

I cannot say it

                the list changes

                                        the images will settle

                all these tubes

                        the program

                        notes

                        say nothing of this

wait

  you can

I can take you here

                    slightest parting

                                  all that already exists

	1	2	3	4	5	6	7	8	9
						from wall to wall			
	it's possible								
							measures		
	there is space								
							numbers		
							tonal variations		
							percussion		
							electronic equivalencies		
								it's clear	

```
                I only have to find

        the oblique muscles

                                the space

        the lungs
        the arms

    all my arms

    I have no more shoulders

                                I feel present
    my head



                    without the mirror


I can

pull


                    the curtain
```

| 1 | 2 | 3 | 4 | 5 | 6 | 7 | 8 | 9 |

these folds

yes

rhythmic lines

you see

an opening

beneath the ribs

it's open

give me

some water

there is no more wall

space between bodies
creates
distance

	1	2	3	4	5	6	7	8	9
you can									
		wait							
I take you									
							I am not afraid		
							of parasites		
							quite the opposite		
		I need							
		air							
you feel									
			a drop in pressure						
in your body									
							sforzando		

39

```
  1    2    3    4    5    6    7    8    9
```

                            it's physiological

                                            it's living

            I'm short of breath

            I'm dizzy

                                    there

yes

                                            to take risks

                                    yes

            I'm losing sight of you

	1	2	3	4	5	6	7	8	9

                              thousands of resting cells

you can let go

                                                                   it's cellular

                                                                         exactly

                                  turning me to liquid

                                                                         one

             I can see you no longer

                                                                           further

                                                                         two

I am there

           where I am

                                                                           close

                                                                         while staying distant

```
      1     2     3     4     5     6     7     8     9

              extended

                                                    outpouring

let me do it

                                              from two
                                                to four




                      tongue
                                  as though I had no more spine

                    to the roof

                    of the mouth


                                        floor touching floor


you listen to me


          I listen to the floor


              pelvic floor
```

45

                                        what this makes possible

                                        an immense opening

                        on the inside

                        I tremble

                                        a capacious

                                        sequence

                                                matter

I can withdraw

                                change

                                                from four
                                                to three

1	2	3	4	5	6	7	8	9

take you again
there

by the throat

                                                  tremulous molecules

              there is no non-dancing state
              not
              for anyone

                                          absolutely
                       concretely

                                      I can see everything
                                      I can take everything in

```
         1    2    3    4    5    6    7    8    9


                  between the muscles and the skin


                              lymph

                              intestines




                                        decrescendo




                                        this is not music




                       the brain issues motor commands
                       according to the source


                                   the frequency


from your mouth



I
                                                      between tremors
slip out
```

	1	2	3	4	5	6	7	8	9
					at the same time				
								come in	
		I can							
		now							
								literally	
	you can								
						going			
								together	
		I might not say							
		what							
					I dance				
						with			

1

I come in

from where I leave

I come in

you point to where you want me to enter

I come in

when I come out you know where I was

where I am no longer

in a way

you see

after the gestures

your nerves

one by one

your genes

neurons

I feel you

go ahead

I can take you here

it's possible

there is space

I can

pull

you see

1

beneath the ribs

you can

I take you

you feel

in your body

yes

you can let go

I am there

let me do it

you listen to me

I can withdraw

take you again

there

by the throat

from your mouth

I

slip out

you can

2

between

yes

you do what

what

I want

what

I don't know

what I don't know

what I want

where this still tingles

your actions remain

you see me

across

how

you know

my fragile constitution

what

piano

non piano

what

I like

you know

2

intimate

to this extent

I cannot say it

wait

you can

all my arms

I have no more shoulders

my head

yes

give me

some water

wait

I need

air

I'm short of breath

I'm dizzy

I'm losing sight of you

I can see you no longer

where I am

extended

I listen to the floor

I can

2

now

I might not say

what

3

marks

mirror

limbs

this involves

a charge

biomechanical

non-isometrical

the oblique muscles

the lungs

the arms

a drop in pressure

thousands of resting cells

tongue

to the roof

of the mouth

pelvic floor

there is no non-dancing state

not

for anyone

between the muscles and the skin

the brain issues motor commands

according to the source

in my tubes

elastic

openings

hypersensitive

shining

localized

this heat persists

spaces tremble

the skin also trembles

intermittently

the entire skeleton

the flesh

under the nails

under the eyelids

other tubes

electric surfaces

immersed

as deeply

as withdrawn

under the membranes

contractions

turbulence

the list changes

all these tubes

these folds

it's physiological

turning me to liquid

as though I had no more spine

on the inside

I tremble

concretely

lymph

intestines

at the same time

I dance

6

scale variations

gestures

fictions

radiance

telescoping

bright zones

X

slightest parting

from wall to wall

without the mirror

the curtain

it's open

there is no more wall

floor touching floor

change

the frequency

going

with

I can't see

the key

pulsing

internally

columns of air

reflexes

sonorous volumes

aberrations

bereft of the instrument

the program

notes

say nothing of this

measures

numbers

tonal variations

percussion

electronic equivalencies

rhythmic lines

an opening

sforzando

there

yes

it's cellular

what this makes possible

an immense opening

a capacious

sequence

tremulous molecules

decrescendo

this is not music

8

I can show you
entrances
sensitive limits
deep in walking
trembling
if we can do it
if we like
go together
deeds
unknown to me
implicit nudity
relentlessly
I can see
persistence
I want to see everything
what this involves
the images will settle
all that already exists
it's clear
I only have to find
the space
space between bodies
creates

distance

I am not afraid

of parasites

quite the opposite

it's living

to take risks

exactly

one

further

two

close

while staying distant

from two

to four

matter

from four

to three

absolutely

I can see everything

I can take everything in

literally

together

tubes

there

I see

bodily

corridors

needles

red

every limb

particles

of the whole

all

these fluid lines

the sounds

I feel present

outpouring

between tremors

come in

NOTE ON THE TEXT

There is no word to designate creation. There are only ellipses. So how to put into words the gestures conceived on the floor, on the bed, on the stage, in the dance? What is a stage if not a playing field delimited by a shared pact in the wager of creation, where mutual consent between individuals upstream renders all experiments possible downstream? Arising not from transgression but assent, through conditions that support disinhibition and exploration: "the body's potential" and its "joyous passions" – Spinoza. How to put into words the movement of a dancing body and/or the relationship between dancing bodies? *Coït* breaks down etymologically as *ire, cum,* "to go with"; in the process of writing *Coït,* I literally *went with* the world. I went to the rehearsal spaces of live performances where I scripted the artists' work, taking notes on what dancers, choreographers, composers and other interlocutors said. I wrote the language down immediately, words born with gestures in the presence of moving and thinking bodies. Then I relocated to my desk and chose from the words. Everything moves: the meanings of words, blood in the veins, minerals, salts and iron, water, our neurons, our organs, our gazes, the air of our breath, our thoughts and affections. In *Coït,* nine tubes – appearing on the page as columns – hold these elements. The tubes are spaces from which one or many bodies speak. The tubes are currents of air where bodies and words can move, resonate, vibrate, irradiate or fade. The nine tubes are nine states or positions, nine dimensions for experimentation: 1) an unwavering, vigorous presence; 2) an offering or acquiescence to abandonment; 3) biological science,

anatomically minimal; 4) the void; 5) interior physiological awareness or vision; 6) the stage set or architectonic materiality; 7) the sonorous or undulatory; 8) anterior vision or intuition, orchestration of an ensemble; 9) action and passion of the witness. There are also nine orifices in the human body.

The double scoring of *Coït* is one, simultaneous writing. As I worked, I wrote the nine tubes considering not only the vertical axis but also how the words accompanied each other horizontally and diagonally. To write the tubes and see them clearly – to read them – I used the spreadsheet program Excel where constraints on manipulation – and related vexations – paradoxically gave me tone, focus, and clarity of mind. From this grew a sort of freedom to concentrate on the composition and reduction work that forms the core of my practice: minimal textual economy to generate maximal polysemous variation.

– Chantal Neveu

MONTRÉAL 2012

An earlier version of Chantal Neveu's *coït* was adapted for radio in a production entitled *Danse/Tanz*, directed by Chantal Dumas and produced by Goetz Naleppa – DeutschlandRadio Kultur Berlin – for the show *Klangkunst*. It was first broadcast on May 6, 2005.

BY CHANTAL NEVEU

èdres, É = É, 2005.

mentale, La Peuplade, 2008.

Une spectaculaire influence, L'Hexagone, 2010.

coït, La Peuplade, 2010.

Je suis venue faire l'amour, Contre-mur, 2010.

Laboratoire parcellaire (collectif), La Peuplade/Oboro, 2011.

IN COLLABORATION (compact disc)

Concret, OHM éditions, 2003 (with composer Georges Azzaria).

èdres | Dehors, É = É, 2005 (with composer Stéphane Claude).

BY ANGELA CARR

ropewalk, Snare Books, 2006.

The Rose Concordance, BookThug, 2009.

Colophon

Manufactured as the First English Edition of *Coït*
by BookThug in the fall of 2012.

Distributed in Canada by the Literary Press Group: www.lpg.ca.
Distributed in the USA by Small Press Distribution: www.spdbooks.org.

Shop online at www.bookthug.ca